THE BOOK OF NIGHTMARES

A FIENDISH GUIDE TO YOUR SCARY DREAMS

Phyllis Raybin Emert

Illustrations: Matt Nelson

LOWELL HOUSE JUVENILE

LOS ANGELES

CONTEMPORARY BOOKS

CHICAGO

Cover illustration by Stephen Johnson

Library of Congress number is available.

ISBN: 1-56565-618-0

Publisher: Jack Artenstein
Director of Publishing Services: Rena Copperman
Editor in Chief, Roxbury Park Books: Michael Artenstein
Managing Editor: Lindsey Hay
Art Director: Lisa-Theresa Lenthall

Roxbury Park is an imprint of Lowell House,
A Division of the RGA Publishing Group, Inc.

Lowell House books can be purchased at special discounts when ordered in bulk for premiums and special sales.
Contact Department TC at the following address:

Lowell House Juvenile
2020 Avenue of the Stars
Suite 300
Los Angeles, CA 90067

Manufactured in the United States of America

10 9 8 7 6 5 4 3 2

Special thanks to:

Barbara Wheeler, Karen Brown, and Carol Huber, their fifth and sixth grade students at Hermosa School, Alta Loma, CA, and

Jason Babineau
Joseph Baddour
Kristina Baird
Danny Belko
Sean Courey-Pickering
Sara Curry
Anthony Keithley
Kevin Korb
Christopher Kunkel
Whitney Low
Brandon O'Harrow
Russell Pitts
Sara Rodriguez
Shenan L. Roethe
Michael J. Santuci
Kristi Shinkle

Contents

Introduction

It is a stormy, windswept night. You are alone in your house, waiting for your parents to come back from a PTA meeting. The lights flicker. "Oh, great," you mumble, "not a blackout," and decide to get a flashlight. As you rise from the sofa, a sudden burst of lightning flashes against the sky and the lights go out.

A booming thunderclap ushers you into a world of darkness. You hear footsteps outside. Is it your parents? No. The footsteps are slow, heavy, like they belong to something big. They get louder—closer—until they stop right outside the window. You know you shouldn't look. You know you'll be sorry if you do. But you just can't help it. You pull back the curtain with a trembling hand.

CRASH! Lightning flashes again and for a moment you see a face, ghostly white with sunken eyes, staring back at you.

You whirl around and notice that the front door is unlocked. As you sprint toward it, you hear the thing outside lumbering across the ground, following you.

You reach for the lock, but the doorknob is already turning.

"Noooooooo . . ."

Suddenly you come awake. You sit bolt upright in the dark of your bedroom, panting, barely able to draw a breath. You've never felt such relief.

It was just a horrible nightmare.

Everyone, young and old, has nightmares. Some are so disturbing that people remember them for many years. Others occur repeatedly. Still others are just shrugged off and forgotten.

A nightmare isn't simply a bad dream; it's an experience that leaves you terrified, frightened, and in distress. This book will cover everything we know about nightmares, including common nightmares and what they mean; nightmares and brain function; nightmares that have come true; as well as a variety of other nightmarish information.

Although nightmares can be scary and disturbing for many people, they can often help us learn more about ourselves.

So, to learn more about these terrifying dreams called nightmares, read on—if you dare. . . .

Nightmares—Who, What, When, How, and Why?

O God, I could be bounded in a nutshell,
and count myself a king of infinite space,
were it not that I have bad dreams.

—Hamlet, *William Shakespeare*

More than a quarter of our lives is spent sleeping. For most people, sleep is a refreshing and relaxing experience. But for millions of people who suffer from continuing nightmares, it is a time of anxiety and terror. Research shows that at least twelve million people have one or more nightmares per week and that most of these people are children.

Nightmares of danger, fear, and death are so common that some psychologists see them as a natural part of development and maturity. Both males and females experience nightmares with equal frequency, usually beginning between the ages of three and six with dreams of scary animals, such as bears and wolves. By age seven or eight we begin to see ghosts, skeletons, monsters, and other supernatural beings in our nightmares.

By age nine or ten our nightmares often involve being chased, kidnapped, attacked, and even murdered. As we mature, we continue to have these nightmares, as well as scary dreams that involve the fears and worries of our daily lives. For older children this may include nightmares about school, exams, sports, career choices, or social life.

Though both males and females have about the same number of nightmares, the content of these bad dreams is usually quite different. Males typically dream in black and white and often have nightmares about dominance, competition, and confronting other males.

REAL NIGHTMARES

I went swimming in our pool. I was in there about five minutes when all these leaves started falling in and a snake slithered into the water. I was trying to get out, but the water kept getting higher and higher.

Just then 50 snakes got into the water and came toward me. They were an inch away when I started screaming, and finally I woke up.

Michael Santuci, 12 years old

One psychiatric study revealed that females, who are often victims in their bad dreams, feel more intense emotions in their nightmares, many of which frequently deal with issues of the home and family.

Nightmares occur most often in times of stress or illness. It's not unusual to have more nightmares during an attack of the flu or in the middle of finals week. Both children and adults have reported more nightmares during high fevers and operations, but it's not clear whether the illness itself or the stress that accompanies the illness is the cause of the nightmares.

Children and adults who have had horrible or particularly frightening experiences often have a higher incidence of nightmares after the terrifying event. These are called *post-traumatic* nightmares and commonly occur in burn, accident, kidnapping, or crime victims.

According to some researchers, adults who suffer chronic nightmares tend to be more artistic, creative, and sensitive than other people. Ernest Hartmann, author of *The Nightmare: The Psychology and Biology of Terrifying Dreams,* concluded that nightmare sufferers are more open and trusting than most people and tend to be more sensitive to their surroundings. They're easily hurt and often let things bother them, so normal fears and angers become more frightening for them than for other people.

? Do Blind People Dream? What Do They See?

Disabled people experience nightmares differently. People who are born blind and those who lost their sight in early childhood do not have visual nightmares like other people. Rather, they hear and feel the terror in darkness. Whatever the disability, the remaining senses heighten the frightening effect.

While much about nightmares remains unknown, one thing is certain: Most children and adults have experienced nightmares, some more often than others, and facing our worst nightmares may prove to be more than scary. It can be useful and even exciting.

The area of sleep science and medicine is a relatively new field. In the early 1950s researchers first discovered two separate types of sleep, identified by the presence or absence of unusual eye movements. REM (rapid-eye-movement) sleep, characterized by erratic eye flickering, became known as dream sleep. The other type of sleep, NREM, is known as non-REM sleep, when the eyes are still and dreams do not occur. Both types of sleep can be monitored by an EEG (electroencephalogram), a machine that measures brain waves.

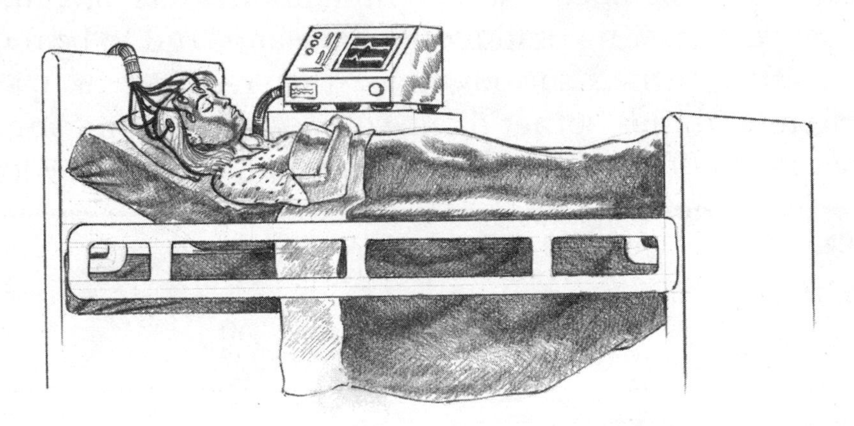

NREM sleep is characterized by even breathing, a steady pulse rate, some body movement, and sometimes snoring. When awakened during NREM sleep, most people cannot remember any nightmares at all.

During REM sleep, however, brain activity increases and heart rate and blood pressure rise. Although the body seems paralyzed, face muscles and fingers may twitch and the eyes move around rapidly under the lids. This is when nightmares take place.

There are four stages of NREM sleep in the first half of the night. Stage 1, the lightest stage, occurs as the subject falls asleep and progresses through Stages 2 and 3, and finally to Stage 4, the deepest sleep stage. Then REM sleep occurs and continues throughout the night following periods of NREM sleep. An entire NREM/REM cycle lasts about 90 minutes.

The first REM phase may only last 10 minutes before another NREM cycle begins. Gradually the REM phases lengthen throughout the night up to an hour or more. Nightmares occur in REM phases during the last half of the night and early in the morning upon awakening, when REM cycles are at their longest.

When awakened during REM sleep, most people are able to describe the nightmares they had in great detail.

The average person has four to five dreams or nightmares each night, the first lasting only a few minutes, while the final dream lasts much longer, particularly if it's a nightmare.

Read on to discover some of the most common and terrifying nightmares that will haunt your sleep!

?

Does Everyone Dream?

Yes. If you don't remember your dreams in the morning, it's probably because you've woken up during NREM sleep. People who claim they never dream are mistaken. They just wake up in the wrong sleep stage!

Common Nightmares and What They Mean

Nightmares have been interpreted in a variety of ways throughout history. Their interpretation might be literal (exactly what they seem to mean), or they may hold some symbolic significance for the dreamer. For example, when someone has a nightmare of the death of a parent, it may actually represent the dreamer's fear that her parents will suddenly leave or stop loving her.

One of the very first books about nightmares and what they mean was written by the Roman scholar Artemidorus. He wrote that each nightmare should be interpreted only after considering the facts of each person's life, personality, occupation, and character. In other words, nightmares mean different things to different people.

This interpretation of dreams and nightmares provided the basis for Dr. Sigmund Freud's ideas on psychoanalysis (or the way a psychologist or psychiatrist analyzes a person's mental well-being), which dominated dream therapy for years. Freud believed that all nightmares contained a hidden theme of wish fulfillment. Whether it was obvious or disguised by symbolism, the object of the dream was something the dreamer wished for.

Some of Freud's own students disagreed with this idea. One of them, Carl Jung (pronounced "Yoong"), became an authority on the subject of dreams and nightmares. Jung did not view dreams and nightmares as wish fulfillment. Rather, he believed they represented parts of one's inner life, a sort of "self-portrait" of the dreamer.

Nightmares, according to Jung, dealt with the dark side of the self, called "the shadow." In such dreams, the shadow is portrayed as a monster or another frightening figure.

Today, many books on dream and nightmare interpretation try to generalize the meaning of nightmares so they can apply to everyone. But the real meaning of a nightmare depends on the personal details of each one and how it relates specifically to the dreamer.

Wish fulfillment? Self-discovery? Personal factors? What do your nightmares tell you about yourself? Only you have the answers. The following examples are common nightmares, variations of which have been dreamed by millions of sleepers. You will probably recognize a few of them.

Nightmares of Being Chased or Attacked

It was a beautiful Saturday morning, but as the day went on, the sky turned gray and gloomy. Everyone went inside their house except me. I had to go to the grocery store.

On my way there, I noticed a man following me. He was dressed in all black and if I turned a corner, he did, too. Then I saw him pull out a knife! He chased me into a corner and was about to dig the knife into me [when] I woke up.

Chris Ybarra, 11 years old

A nightmare of being chased, stalked, or attacked is often considered the result of anxiety and fear. It may be triggered by a frightening real-life incident, a scary movie that had similar scenes, or even hearing about some event on the evening news.

Some analysts believe these types of nightmares are projections of one's own anger or hostility toward someone or something. Instead of being the attacker in the nightmare, the dreamer projects him or herself as the victim of the attack. For example, if you're very angry at a friend or a relative in real life, you may be the victim of an attack by that friend or relative in your nightmare.

After experiencing one of these nightmares, see if it matches up with a time in your life when you were angry or upset with others. Analyze the details of the dream and see how they relate to you personally. Have you had a nightmare in which your teacher is chasing you with a ruler in his hand? Perhaps it's because you happen to be behind on your homework in that particular class, or the teacher caught you passing notes to another student. The attacker in the nightmare may represent something or someone that is bothering you in your daily life. Then again, the nightmare may just be a replay of a scene from that horror movie you watched the other night!

Nightmares of Water

My family and I went to a big blue lake to fish. My dad and brother jumped in with a splash with about 10 other people. All of a sudden, my brother screamed a blood-curdling scream and got pulled down, under the lake.

My dad immediately jumped under the water to get him back. I was frozen in shock and I started [to] run away as fast as I could to my mom.

We [ran back to] the area and I dived under the water to get my brother. Then I saw it—a shark as big as a bus and heading straight for me! I saw my brother and dad ripped to pieces and I screamed and screamed and screamed.

Christy Cavanaugh, 12 years old

Traditionally, large bodies of water, like oceans and lakes, have been interpreted as symbols for the unconscious mind, or the part of the psyche that people are not aware of. Some people believe water nightmares reflect the dreamer's unconscious feelings or conflicts, which he or she doesn't even know about. If this is true, water nightmares are the answer to the question "What's on your mind?" whether you're thinking it or not.

For example, you have a nightmare in which you are in a canoe drifting on a vast ocean. You are hopelessly lost and need help. Does this nightmare relate to your real life? Do you feel lost in math class? Are you new in school and feel nervous about being in a place you don't know? Your actions in relation to the water are significant. Will you fight against the rising water or accept your fate? Will the water cleanse you so that you can be reborn and make a new start in life? What does the water represent to you personally? Danger, peace, fun? Is it your subconscious mind, or are you just awfully thirsty? Only you have the answers!

Nightmares of Falling

I was running. The ground under me was wet. My feet made a pat, pat [sound] on the ground. I looked behind me. All I saw was a shadow. My feet felt air. I looked down: a cliff! My heart gave a leap. I tumbled down in a big black abyss.

I woke up and I was falling down to the ground. I sat up and looked around. I had fallen from my bunk bed!

Matt Perez, 12 years old

This common nightmare is very disturbing because the sensation of falling from a high place can be very realistic to the dreamer. Some evolutionists (who believe that all living things have developed over time by a gradual process of continuous change) think that the falling nightmare is an ancient memory from our ape and monkey

?

In a Falling Nightmare, If You Hit the Ground, Will You Die?

No! This is an old myth that has no basis in fact. Many people actually land in their dreams without ill effect, though most seem to wake up before they hit bottom. Whether the dreamer lands after a fall may change the meaning of the nightmare, but it will not likely cause any real physical harm.

ancestors, who often fell from the branches of trees. In some instances, it may be a replay of an actual fall that occurred months or even years before. Falling nightmares can even be brought on by toppling out of bed!

In certain cases, a falling nightmare may represent a loss of control or the fear of failure. For instance, the dreamer may be experiencing a fall from power or a falling-out with friends. Falling into empty space may mean a general feeling of loneliness or helplessness in your life.

Details, such as what you are falling away from, or what you are falling toward, may be helpful in interpreting this kind of nightmare.

Nightmares of Death

The first thing I remember in my nightmare was that I was running slowly through a field of enormous yellow sunflowers, searching for my family. I was cold and it started to rain. It was dark and I started to turn around in circles like a hurricane out of control!

That's when the beautiful field of sunflowers turned into a cemetery. There I saw my family by a cold marble tombstone—dead! I was with them, lying there pale and wet. I was frantic and woke up screaming!

Erin Trier, 11 years old

Nightmares about the death of loved ones do not necessarily mean the dreamer wants his or her family to die or be killed. Rather, these nightmares may express fears of abandonment by the family or loss of love and support.

Death nightmares may also reflect the idea that the dreamer is moving apart from the family. Or perhaps the family is holding back the dreamer, and despite anguish and grief, he or she must continue on with life apart from the family.

Some analysts believe the death of a loved one in a nightmare is a form of self-punishment by the dreamer for something he or she feels guilty about. For example, you skip soccer practice one day but feel guilty about it afterward. That night you have a nightmare in which your mother is killed while you are away having fun. Your guilt has probably triggered this nightmare, in which you inflict your own form of self-punishment for skipping practice—the death of your mother.

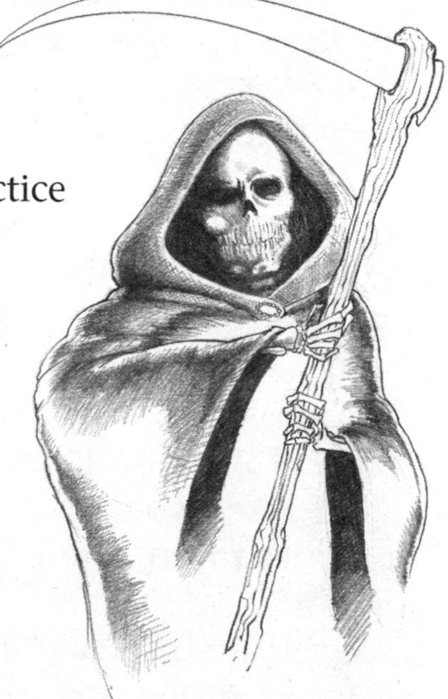

At the same time, death nightmares may also be seen as a turning point in one's life—"death" to the old life, and the start of a new one.

There are many interpretations of this common nightmare. Of course, the one that fits depends on the dreamer.

Nightmares of Disaster

In my nightmare, my family and I were all asleep when our house caught on fire. My brother and I crawled to my parents' room and tried to wake them up. We kept trying and trying to wake them up, but they didn't. At last they woke up.

Then I remembered my two-year-old brother, Austin. I went to his room and tried to get him out, but I could not pick him up. I yelled for my mom and she picked him up. All of us went downstairs.

We couldn't get out because the [door] handles were too hot. I thought we were going to die! Finally I woke up.

Ashlie Jennea Encinias, 10½ years old

Nightmares of disaster, such as earthquakes, fires, or major accidents, are especially common to those who have experienced one or the other and have been terribly frightened by the experience.

Earthquakes are generally considered to be symbolic of Mother Earth or Nature. In interpreting nightmares about earthquakes, you need to focus on what is being shaken up or destroyed and its relationship to you and your personal life.

Surprisingly, dreaming of fire was traditionally considered a good sign. According to Gustavus Hindman Miller in his book *10,000 Dreams Interpreted,* "fire is favorable to the dreamer if he does not get burned," and "to dream of seeing your home burning denotes a loving companion, obedient children, and careful servants."

Then again, a dream of fire or another disaster might be triggered by reading about a similar incident or seeing a movie. In your nightmare about fire, pay particular attention to your own actions. Do you rescue someone? Do you get burned? Details such as whether you are in control of the situation or it controls you are significant in interpreting the meaning of fire and other disaster nightmares.

Nightmares in which you are not in control may be a warning that you need to be more assertive with your friends and family. Your nightmares may be telling you to take command of your life.

Nightmares of Animals and Bugs

My leg was itching real bad, and then I saw all these spiders crawling up. I started to scream, but nothing came out . . . I ran to get the hose . . . My grandma stopped me and asked me where I was going . . . I told her, but she wouldn't move. Then her white-colored face started to turn a black color . . . Her hand turned black and she grew three more arms on each side. Before I knew it, she was a spider!

Then everyone else I knew turned into hideous black widows. They started to crawl on me and bite. Before I knew it, I was on the ground half dead. Then I woke up.

Robert Price, 13 years old

In nightmares about insects, the bugs generally represent daily problems and worries. Whether you take action to eliminate the pests in your nightmare or allow them to gain control over you are crucial factors in interpreting the meaning of this type of nightmare.

Larger animals may represent a number of things. A wild animal, such as a lion or a tiger, is probably a symbol. In interpreting these kinds of animal nightmares, analyze the relationship between you and the animal. Were you frightened? Was the animal in control of the situation? If so, what person or thing in real life might it represent that is controlling you? Or could the wild beast in your nightmare signify the animal part of your personality, as Jung suggested? Only you have the answers!

Nightmares of Paralysis

I was outside playing with my sister when suddenly a man and woman walked up to us. My sister and I were too frightened to move. We were like frozen ice cubes in the freezer. Our hearts were pounding harder and harder.

The man was standing behind me with a gun in his hand. The gun was pointing right at me, and I couldn't move!

Britni Clark, 11 years old

This common nightmare is one of the most frightening and usually means the dreamer is in conflict about something and is experiencing a feeling of indecision or helplessness. Is there a situation in your daily life in which you can't make an important decision? Look carefully at the details of your personal life in interpreting paralysis nightmares. Take control and face whatever is threatening you, and you may find it's not nearly as bad as your nightmare!

It's interesting to note that in nightmares in which the dreamer is unable to move, run, scream, or get away from a threatening situation, it is quite true that he or she really *cannot* move or scream. Remember that dreams occur in REM sleep, when, except for occasional hand or mouth twitching, the dreamer really is paralyzed!

Nightmares of Nudity

I had to present a report to my class. I walked to the front of the room, turned to face the class, and everyone began laughing and pointing at me. I looked down and realized that I had forgotten to put on my clothes that morning—I was naked! I ran out of the classroom.

Chris Ives, 12 years old

Most interpretations of the nudity nightmare are symbolic. In other words, the nightmare does not actually mean you are afraid of being seen naked. In this scenario, traipsing around nude may just be a way of getting more attention.

A nudity nightmare may also be a way of expressing openness and honesty with those in the dream. Their response—ridicule and embarrassment—reveals the dreamer's fear of such openness.

Details of such a nightmare, such as the dreamer's feelings about being seen naked and the response of others, are critical in interpreting these frightening—and embarrassing!—nightmares.

Another common nightmare deals with the loss of teeth. Teeth nightmares often seem so real and horrifying that you may find yourself examining your teeth to be sure they're still there when you wake up!

The traditional interpretation of this nightmare links the loss of teeth with dying. In ancient times, losing one's teeth meant not being able to eat properly, which lead to a weakened condition, ill health, weight loss, and eventually death. Artemidorus believed that teeth symbolized the members of one's family. Therefore, the loss of a tooth meant the death of a loved one.

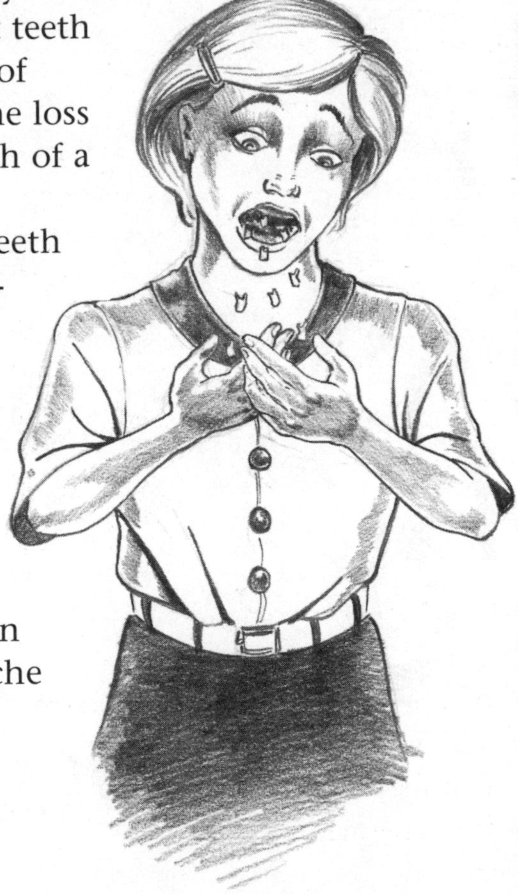

Among older people, teeth nightmares often symbolize a preoccupation with aging, while younger dreamers might equate teeth loss with a feeling of being powerless or helpless. On the other hand, teeth nightmares may simply be brought on by a troublesome toothache or even fear of going to the dentist!

Precognitive Nightmares—Nightmares That Come True

Since biblical times, people have used their nightmares to predict the future and to give warning or knowledge of an event before it actually happens. Such nightmares were believed to be the means God used to communicate with man. They are called *precognitive nightmares,* or premonitions.

In the Bible, it was Joseph's successful interpretation of the pharaoh's troubling nightmares that elevated him from slavery to Prime Minister of Egypt. Joseph said to the pharaoh, "God has revealed to Pharaoh what he is about to do . . . There will come seven years of great plenty throughout the land of Egypt, but after them there will arise seven years of famine. . . ."

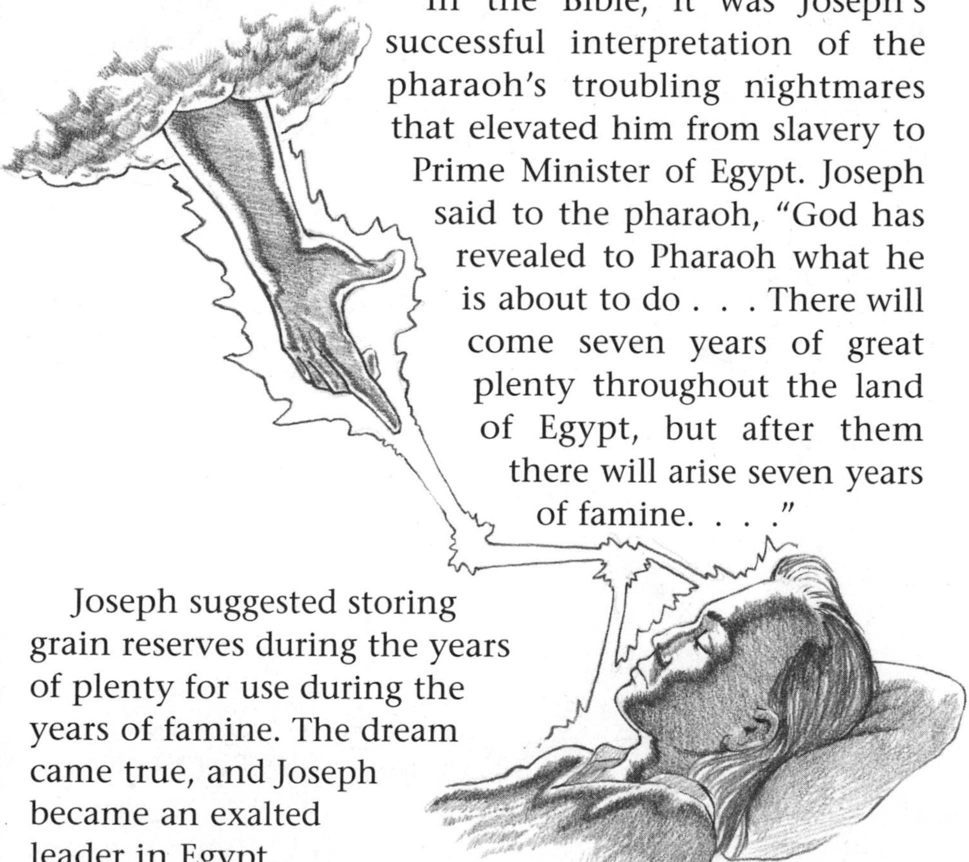

Joseph suggested storing grain reserves during the years of plenty for use during the years of famine. The dream came true, and Joseph became an exalted leader in Egypt.

The Bible is filled with other examples of precognitive dreams. From Nebuchadnezzar to Daniel to Jacob and Elijah, nightmares that came true were looked upon as direct messages from the Almighty.

In modern times, nightmares that genuinely predict the future are often associated with people who have psychic powers or extrasensory perception (ESP). A psychic person is believed to have special abilities and knowledge that extend beyond the normal five senses (sight, hearing, smell, taste, and touch).

However, many precognitive dreams can be explained by coincidence or high probability. For example, if you dream that a relative who has smoked cigarettes heavily for many years will die of lung cancer, ESP isn't necessarily at work, only statistical probability.

Yet there are many nightmares that cannot be explained, and some are quite amazing. Many precognitive nightmares have happened to very famous and reliable people, and others were experienced by ordinary unknowns. Most were shared by the dreamer with others who acted as witnesses to the credibility of the nightmare and the subsequent event that came true.

After Julius Caesar was made dictator of Rome in 44 B.C., a plot against his life was secretly planned. On the night of March 14, his wife, Calpurnia, awoke sobbing after a terrible nightmare. She had dreamed she was holding the bloody dead body of her husband in her arms. Calpurnia begged Caesar not to go to the Senate that day, believing he was in danger. Caesar went anyway and was stabbed to death by those he thought were his friends. Calpurnia's nightmare had come true.

King William II of England, the son and successor of William the Conqueror, shared a nightmare with his hunting companions one morning in 1100 A.D. He dreamed that an icy-cold wind sliced through his body, numbing his flesh. It was a frightening nightmare, and some of the king's companions believed it to be a bad omen. William insisted on continuing the hunt and hours later was killed by an arrow that entered his body under his arm. Whether his death was intentional or an accident, the nightmare had come true.

In June of 1822, the great English romantic poet Percy Shelley had a frightening nightmare in which he drowned. Shelley woke up screaming and told the details of his nightmare to his wife, Mary, and two friends, Jane and Edward Williams, who had hurried into his room. Several weeks later, Shelley and Edward drowned while

sailing on the Bay of Spezia in Italy after a sudden and violent storm overwhelmed Shelley's boat. He was only 30 years old.

Can Nightmares Kill?

There is no proof that nightmares can cause any real physical harm. Many people have reported dying in their nightmares and have experienced no ill effects upon awakening.

In 1873, Rabbi Hile Wechsler of Bavaria, Germany, had a terrible nightmare about a future catastrophe for the Jewish people. The nightmare warned of destruction, horror, and hostility against the Jews on a massive scale. It was so disturbing that Rabbi Wechsler self-published a small pamphlet called "A Word of Warning," predicting the upcoming disaster.

Rabbi Wechsler's pamphlet was published eight years later in 1881. This was more than 40 years before the Nazis gained control in Germany and the Holocaust occurred. Was Wechsler's nightmare a genuine precognitive dream? Judge for yourself.

> *I saw in the East—in the proximity of*
> *Rumania—a terrible thunderstorm,*
> *and from there a mass of threatening*
> *dark clouds moved all around to most*
> *of the European states. But it came to*
> *Germany earlier than to Austria-Hungary . . .*
> *the Rumanian spirit of hostility against the*
> *Jews will make its rounds in other states,*
> *but it will strike roots first in Germany*
> *before it grips other countries . . .*
>
> —Rabbi Hile Wechsler, 1873

Another well-documented case of a precognitive dream occurred in May 1812, when a British man named John Williams had a detailed and frightening nightmare of murder. Williams dreamed he was in the lobby of the House of Commons when he saw a man in a dark coat with metal buttons fire a gun at a man dressed in blue with a white vest. The man in blue was killed instantly.

Someone shouted that Spencer Perceval, the British Prime Minister, had been killed, and Williams woke up at that instant. He described the dream to his wife and had the exact same nightmare twice more that evening when he tried to go back to sleep.

Perceval himself also feared for his life that May. Like Williams, he dreamed that he would be murdered in Parliament by a man wearing a green coat and brass buttons. Perceval told his wife about his terrible nightmare, as well as his friend, the Earl of Harrowby. Despite the nightmare, Perceval went to the House of Commons on May 11, 1812.

That day a man named John Bellingham, who wore a green coat with brass buttons, shot Perceval dead as he walked through the lobby of Parliament! The nightmares of both Williams and Perceval had come true.

Another famous case involved the 16th President of the United States, Abraham Lincoln. Early in April 1865, Lincoln dreamed he woke up late one night in the White House to find everyone in the East Room gathered around a dead body dressed in a suit.

Lincoln asked one of the soldiers stationed in the room who the dead person was.

"The president," the soldier replied. "He was killed by an assassin." Lincoln awoke in a cold sweat and was so haunted by the nightmare that he told his wife and other close friends about it.

Several days later, on April 14, 1865, the Lincolns went to a play at Ford's Theater in Washington. That evening, John Wilkes Booth shot the 56-year-old president in the back of the head with a small handgun. Lincoln was dead by morning and his body was laid out in the East Room of the White House, just like in his nightmare.

One night while still a young man, the famous American writer Mark Twain, or Samuel Clemens, his real name, had a nightmare about his brother, Henry

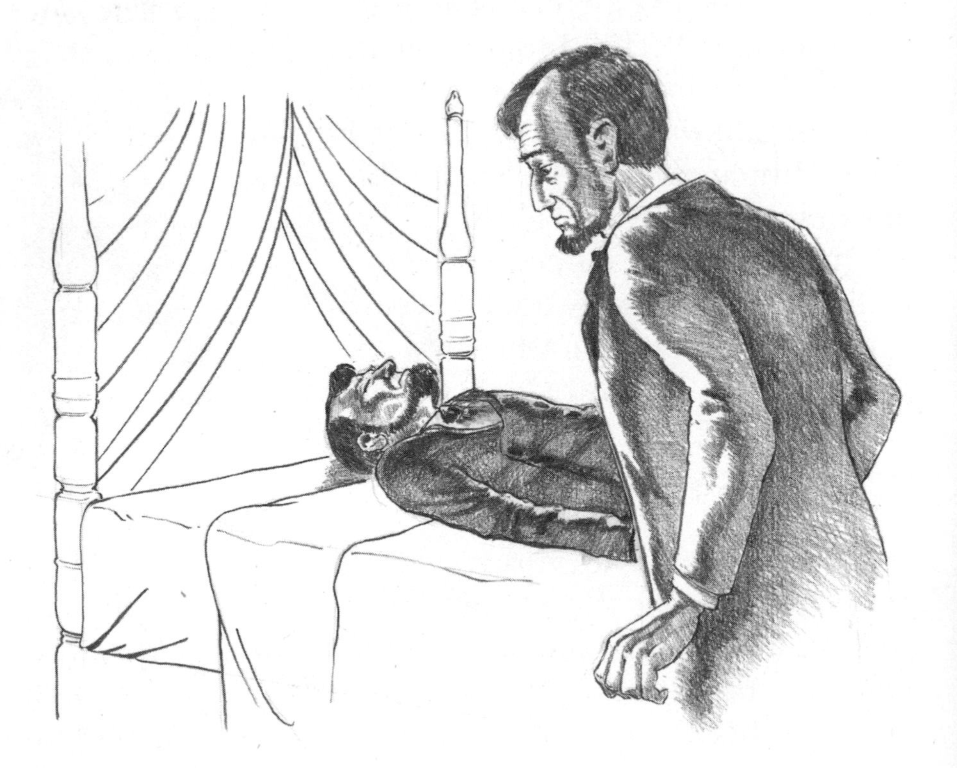

Clemens. Twain dreamed that his brother was dead in a metal coffin that rested on two chairs in his sister's house. On Henry's chest was a bouquet of flowers with a red rose in the center. When Twain woke up, he told his sister about the nightmare and then forgot about it.

The Clemens brothers worked on Mississippi riverboats and traveled the river between St. Louis and New Orleans. Several weeks after the nightmare, the brothers were returning to St. Louis on separate boats when Henry's boat, the *Pennsylvania,* exploded near Memphis, Tennessee, killing 150 people. Henry was severely burned and died several days later. Most of the victims were placed in wooden coffins, but money was donated by local citizens to buy a special metal coffin for Henry, since he was such a young man.

When Mark Twain went to see his brother's body one last time, the scene was exactly like the nightmare, with one difference. The metal coffin rested on two chairs, not at his sister's home in St. Louis, but in a sitting room near Memphis. What about the flowers? As Mark Twain stood near his brother's coffin, a veiled woman entered the room and placed a bouquet on his brother'scoffin. In the middle of the white flower arrangement was a single red rose! Twain strongly believed he had had a precognitive nightmare and throughout his life told others of his strange, unexplained experience.

I was in the jungle, hanging from an unstable vine. I looked below [and saw] ravenous alligators, just waiting for me to fall so they could eat me. The vine snapped!

Then an elephant's trunk wrapped around me, and then it put me down. After a while, shouts arose from the sky. I lost my footing and fell into the alligator pit. . . .

Whitney Low, 10 years old

In a precognitive nightmare, the dreamer tends to be more of an observer than an active participant, as in a typical nightmare. For some reason more women than men have precognitive nightmares, and the nightmares are usually quite detailed and memorable.

The *Titanic* disaster of April 14, 1912, in which the luxury ocean liner sank on its maiden voyage from England to America after hitting an iceberg, is associated with a large number of precognitive nightmares. More than 1,500 people died in the freezing waters of the Atlantic when the *Titanic* went down, with only 20 lifeboats aboard. Seven hundred passengers survived the ordeal.

An English businessman named Middleton had a nightmare of the *Titanic* floating upside down in the ocean with the passengers in the water around it. Middleton was due to sail on the huge ship in less than 10 days when he had the same nightmare again. The nightmare so disturbed him that he told his friends about this recurring experience. The Englishman turned out to be one of the *Titanic's* lucky would-be passengers. His trip was canceled due to business reasons.

Journalist W. T. Stead, who in his writings often warned about the danger of ships that didn't carry enough lifeboats, was himself warned by a psychic friend not to sail on the *Titanic*. Apparently the psychic had a nightmare about the sinking of a large ship with screaming people in the water around it. Stead laughed off the warning and died in the icy Atlantic.

On the night that the "unsinkable" luxury liner hit the iceberg, a woman in America had a nightmare that her mother was in a dangerously crowded lifeboat in the open sea. Her husband reassured her that her mother was safe in England.

The next day, the woman read about the *Titanic* in the newspaper. To her amazement, she saw her mother's name listed as a survivor. She had made the trip to surprise her daughter and spent the night in an overcrowded lifeboat, fearing it would sink along with the ship. Whether this was a genuine precognitive nightmare or an ESP experience of what was taking place thousands of miles away is uncertain, but the nightmare proved to be true.

In 1979, a man named David Booth of Cincinnati, Ohio, had a horrible nightmare in which he saw an American Airlines jetliner roll over in the air, crash to the ground, and explode in flames. The dream was so vivid, its effect so frightening, that Booth couldn't stop thinking about it.

For 10 nights in a row, he had the same awful nightmare until he decided to take action. On May 22, Booth called American Airlines, a professor at a local university, and finally the Federal Aviation Administration (FAA) at the Cincinnati airport to tell them of his nightmare. Although the FAA was sympathetic, they could do nothing to prevent the possibility of a crash short of grounding all American Airlines planes, and that was impossible.

On May 25, 1979, only three days after Booth's call to the FAA, American Airlines Flight 191, en route to Los Angeles from Chicago, lost power after takeoff, rolled over, and crashed in flames. All 272 people on board were killed as well as three on the ground. David Booth's nightmare had come true!

Dr. Hans Holzer, a famous ghost hunter and parapsychologist (someone who studies psychological phenomena, like ESP), wrote about a psychic named Judy Hoffman in *FATE* magazine. Apparently Hoffman told her therapist on August 23, 1994, about a nightmare she had in which she saw a U.S. Air flight taking off for Pittsburgh and bursting into flames.

Hoffman noted that the plane was "not fully repaired," and the therapist wrote the contents of the dream in Hoffman's file.

On September 8, 1994, a U.S. Air 737 bound for Pittsburgh exploded in the air and crashed. Weeks later the manufacturer of the plane, Boeing, admitted in a newspaper article that some 737s were known to be flying with defective parts. Judy Hoffman's nightmare, too, had come true!

Aviation pioneer and author J. T. Dunne had several genuine precognitive nightmares. In each case Dunne's nightmares were authenticated by witnesses he had told before the incidents took place. In 1902, Dunne had a disturbing nightmare in which he knew there would be an eruption of Mont Pelée, a dormant volcano on the island of Martinique in the French West Indies. In the nightmare, Dunne begged French officials to evacuate the 4,000 people on the island. Dunne's nightmare came true hours later when, on May 8, 1902, the Mont Pelée volcano erupted and completely destroyed the town of Saint-Pierre and its 40,000 inhabitants. The only thing

REAL NIGHTMARES

As I was flying in a plane, lightning struck the left wing. The lights went out and everybody on the left vanished. The left emergency door opened, and a man threw everybody a parachute with his left hand and said, "Exit on the left."

Two people were shoving people out the door. The plane was hurtling closer and closer to the ground. I jumped out, pulled my cord, and pots and pans flew out of the top [of the parachute].

Sean Courey-Pickering, 10 years old

about Dunne's premonition that was wrong was the number of lives lost in the disaster.

In another nightmare in 1913, Dunne watched as a train jumped the tracks and crashed over an embankment north of the Firth of Forth Bridge in Scotland. Dunne related the nightmare to his sister, and since he believed that the accident would occur in the spring, he began to warn his friends about traveling over that area by train. Sure enough on April 14, 1914, a mail train called the *Flying Scotsman* derailed and crashed over the exact embankment as in Dunne's nightmare!

There were two dozen proven cases of people who had precognitive nightmares before the Aberfan disaster of December 21, 1966, in South Wales. In this small village a mountain of coal waste rolled down a hillside and buried a school and a number of houses, killing 116 schoolchildren and 28 adults.

One woman dreamed in detail about the coal covering the school and focused on one small boy who seemed to have survived the tragedy. The nightmare was so disturbing that the woman described it in church one day *before* the disaster occurred. More than six witnesses confirmed her story, and the boy depicted in the dream was later seen on television alive and well.

The day before the disaster, a nine-year-old girl described to her mother a nightmare in which her school was no longer there because something black had covered it. The next day, that same girl was one of the victims at Aberfan.

Many nightmares throughout history have come true. Can tragedy be averted if some action is taken after such precognitive nightmares? Read on! The following examples are of people who took action to prevent the events in their precognitive nightmares.

One woman visiting Atlantic City with her niece in the late 1800s had a horrible nightmare in which she was burned alive in a hotel fire. The nightmare was so frightening that the woman took her niece and returned to her home in Philadelphia immediately. The very next day, the hotel burned to the ground along with 10 others in Atlantic City.

The woman who changed her actions as a result of her precognitive nightmare was Susan B. Anthony (1820–1906), co-leader, along with Elizabeth Cady Stanton, of the women's suffrage movement in America. Her actions saved her life, and possibly ensured the future voting rights of American women. However, the tragic fire still took place, and the inevitable disaster could not be averted.

Another historical figure acted after having a precognitive nightmare and saved his life, affecting the future of millions of people. A German soldier in a trench in World War I had a particularly terrible nightmare one evening in November 1917. He dreamed that he was buried alive in the earth and was choking to death. The young soldier awoke gasping for air. Everything seemed calm around him, but he went for a walk anyway to settle his nerves. He left the protection of the trench and walked for several minutes. Suddenly gunfire erupted and an enemy shell exploded near the soldier. Seeing how exposed he was in the open field, the young man ran back to the trench. He was shocked to see that all that remained was dirt and debris. The shell had scored a direct hit on the trench, bringing down tons of earth on the sleeping German soldiers. The soldier's terrible nightmare had come true, but he had saved his own life by going for the walk. The young German's name was Adolph Hitler, and he lived to become one of the most despised men in history.

Ordinary people have also changed their behavior as a result of their precognitive nightmares. During World War I, a woman dreamed that the ship on which her husband was supposed to sail for India was hit by a torpedo and sank. In the dream her husband was alive but badly injured. As a result of the nightmare, the woman begged her husband not to leave on the ship and became so upset that he got permission to be excused from the voyage. Three weeks later, the ship was indeed torpedoed and sunk!

In another case a young mother had a nightmare in which the chandelier over her baby's crib fell and crushed the infant to death. The dream was so horrible that to be on the safe side, the woman took her baby out of the crib

to sleep next to her in the master bedroom. Hours later, a loud crash awakened the family. The chandelier had crashed down on the crib, breaking it into pieces. The baby was safe because of the mother's nightmare.

These frightening nightmares did come true, yet the danger to the people in question was avoided, due to the dreamer's reactions. In effect, the nightmares served as an early warning sign to these particular individuals.

Such precognitive nightmares and premonitions remain unexplained mysteries and are the objects of continuing research and study, even on the Internet. For example, you can write to psychologist Yaron Mayer at the Central Premonitions Registry (at http://clever.net/yaron/precog/precog.htm) with any precognitive dreams or nightmares you might have—and then sit back and see if they come true!

Nightmares in Other Cultures

Nightmares mean different things to different peoples and cultures throughout the world. One particular people, the Senoi, who live in the equatorial rain forest of the Central Range of the Malay Peninsula, have built their entire community life upon a system of nightmare psychology. This isolated jungle tribe is noted for its complete absence of violent crime, armed conflict, mental illness, and physical disease. The tribe was first brought to the world's attention by anthropologist Kilton Stewart.

Stewart lived with the Senoi for one year in 1935 and wrote about their methods of nightmare psychology and interpersonal relationships. Although the Senoi are considered a primitive culture by Western standards, the methods they use to maintain their crime-free society are more sophisticated and successful than in many Western countries. Stewart believed that all people could profit by studying the Senoi's methods.

The major authority figures in Senoi society are called *halaks,* similar to psychologists in Western cultures. A *tohat* is a highly esteemed Senoi who is both a healer and an educator among the halaks. These are the people who help to interpret Senoi nightmares.

In a typical Senoi family, the day begins by having the children relate their dreams and nightmares of the night before to the older adult males, who listen carefully and analyze them. Later, the men gather in the community council to discuss and analyze the dreams and nightmares of the adults.

The Senoi believe that every person can control the forces and beings in his or her dream universe by whatever actions they have taken during the daytime. Thus, if a person has treated his or her friends and neighbors well in his or her daily life, he or she can demand and receive their help and support in his or her dream universe.

Senois are taught from an early age to take control of their nightmares. Instead of running away in fear, they are taught to turn and face the unknown danger. If a Senoi is attacked by someone or something in a nightmare, he or she is encouraged to fight back until friends or neighbors come to help him or her. The dreamer must always take an active part in the nightmare, face any danger, and overcome it.

Stewart wrote that many Senoi children are terrified by falling nightmares. Instead of the adult comforting the child, as in Western culture, the Senoi adult praises the child for having such a wonderful dream, one of the best anyone could hope to have. The Senoi adult asks the child where he or she fell and what he or she learned about the fall, and explains that everything a person does in a nightmare has a purpose.

Consistent advice and praise for the Senoi child after each nightmare slowly change the child's fear and anxiety to relaxation and comfort. According to Stewart, the fear of falling gradually becomes the joy of flying.

If there are hostilities or bad feelings in a nightmare toward another person, the dreamer, upon awakening, is encouraged to go to that person and be friendly in order to counteract the bad feelings of the nightmare.

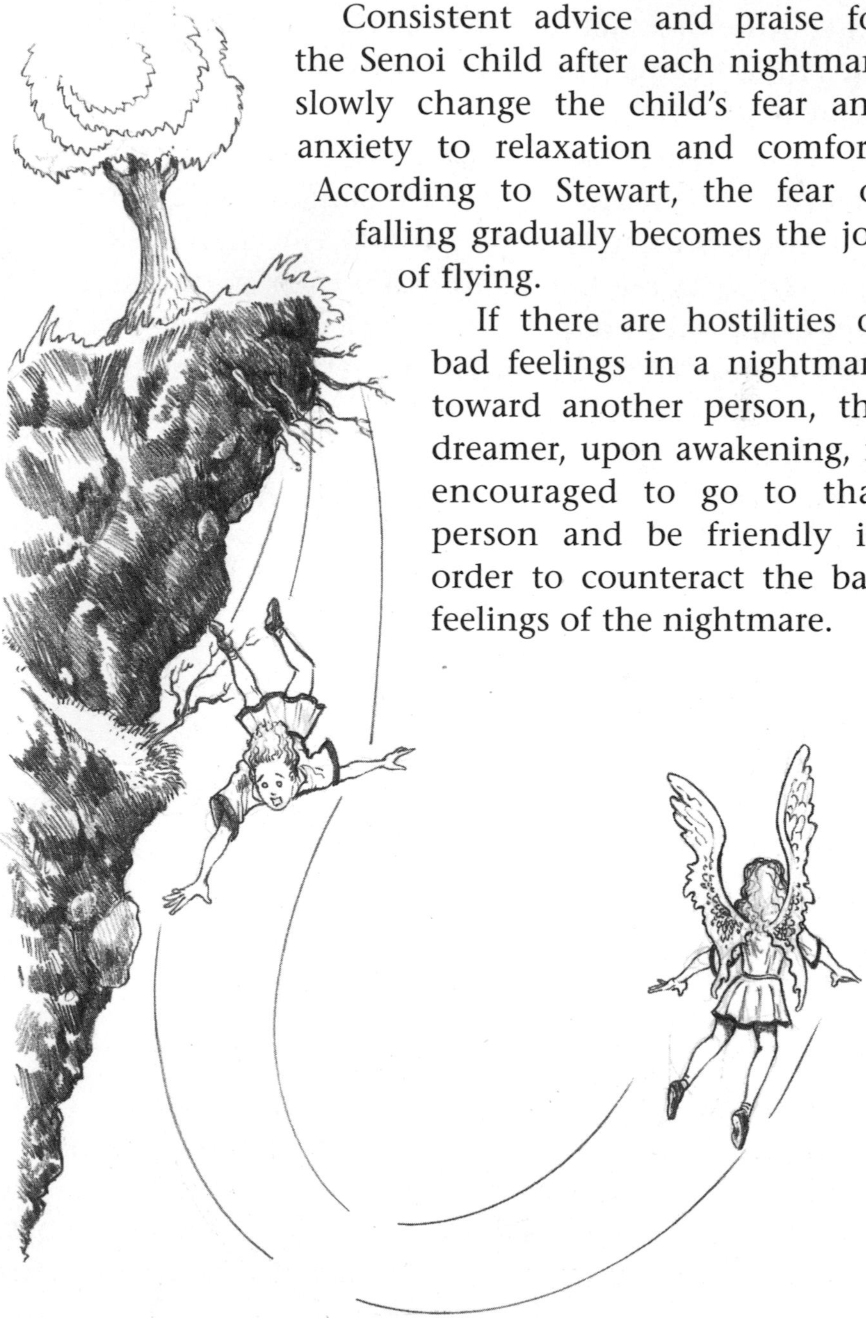

Stewart gave an example of a Senoi child who dreams he is attacked by a friend. He tells the friend of the nightmare, and in turn, the friend is encouraged to give a present to the dreamer and be especially friendly to him. If the child dreams he attacks his friend, upon awakening, he apologizes and brings his friend a present. Thus, any aggression reflected in a nightmare is quickly diffused in the waking world by friendly exchanges and sharing. This concept applies to all Senoi, adults as well as children.

The Senois are taught to share their nightmares with others and take control and direct the outcome of these nightmares. They are taught to relax during the nightmares, to assume a responsible attitude toward what occurs within them, and make a constructive and useful contribution to the society after awakening.

Many cultures make no distinction at all between nightmares and reality.

The Kai tribe of New Guinea, the Pokomams of Guatemala, and the Ashantis of West Africa, among others, believe that a person must be punished in real life for any crime committed during a nightmare. They believe that nightmares are caused by actions committed by the dreamer's soul, which leaves the body at night during sleep.

For example, if anyone learns that an Ashanti man has had a nightmare in which he committed a crime against a neighbor, he must compensate the neighbor or accept punishment, since his soul was guilty of the crime. However, if no one hears of the nightmare, the man may go to an area in the village equivalent to the garbage dump, where he can

get get rid of the nightmare by whispering, "I have dreamed an evil nightmare. Grant that it may never happen like that."

Within these cultures, everything in a nightmare is believable. It is impossible to deny any crime or wrongdoing in a nightmare, because the act was presumably committed by the soul while the person was asleep. If a native of Paraguay or Borneo has a nightmare in which an acquaintance steals or murders his livestock, the acquaintance is considered guilty of the crime. The testimony of a nightmare is stronger than a denial by the accused.

Some cultures give an opposite meaning to their nightmares. The Maoris of New Zealand and the Zulus of Africa believe if someone dies in a nightmare, that person will recover and live, but to dream of a birth means someone will die. In these societies, horrible nightmares are preferable to pleasant dreams, since the reverse will supposedly come true.

Many Native American cultures used nightmares and dreams to shape every facet of their tribal lives. Experiences in the spiritual world of nightmares were taken very seriously. A Native American who had a nightmare of being bitten by a poisonous snake or who contracted a serious disease would, upon waking, seek immediate treatment from a healer of the tribe.

The Iroquois tribe of New York State placed a greater emphasis on the dream world than the waking world, which was of secondary importance to them. Their reality was the dream, and they followed it in every detail.

The Iroquois believed the desires revealed in an individual's dreams and nightmares should be granted in the waking world to prevent illness or bad feelings. If an

Iroquois had a nightmare in which he stalked and murdered a wild beast, he would immediately act out the dream to please what was assumed to be his soul's desire.

Cultural beliefs influence how different people throughout the world deal with their nightmares. In the Western world, nightmares are often considered insignificant. They are feared and ignored, with the hope that they will go away.

However, some Western therapists today are using techniques similar to those of the Senoi, especially when working with young children. Instead of ignoring the nightmare, a child is urged to face up to the monster and learn to be the master of his or her own nightmare. The children are learning to face the terror and overcome the fear.

Nightmares of Invention and Inspiration

Nightmares often leave people terrified, frightened, and upset. But for some inventors, writers, musicians, and philosophers, nightmares have served as creative inspirations for some of their finest works.

It was a nightmare that allowed Elias Howe (1819–1867) to invent the sewing machine. Howe had been working for years on the machine, but the needle design didn't perform properly. One night in 1844, Howe dreamed he was captured by a band of savages whose king commanded him to finish the machine. When he couldn't, the king sentenced Howe to death. Just before his execution, Howe noticed the eye-shaped holes on the spears of the warriors.

Awaking abruptly from the nightmare, he recalled the holes in the spears and decided to use the eye-shaped holes as the basis for the needle design for his invention. The design worked, and the first successful sewing machine came into existence.

Do Animals Dream?

Almost all animals experience REM sleep. However, the dreams of animals lack the structure of human dreams and nightmares and are likely to be of memories of past experiences. For example, if your cat whines in her sleep, she may be having a nightmare of when she was chased by the neighborhood dog!

René Descartes (pronounced "day-CART") was a 15th century French mathematician often called the father of modern philosophy (the study of the principles or truths of a particular branch of knowledge). He credited a series of nightmares with inspiring his methods of philosophical thought.

Descartes experienced the first two nightmares on the night of November 10, 1619. In the first nightmare, a devilish wind flung Descartes around violently, causing him physical pain and weakness. The second nightmare was filled with frightening claps of thunder and ear-piercing noises that so terrified the mathematician that he awoke in fear.

In his third dream, Descartes was reading a dictionary and collection of poems at the same time. This last dream made him think of a connection between philosophy (symbolized by the poetry book) and the sciences (symbolized by the dictionary).

For the remainder of his life, Descartes wrote about applying the scientific methods of experiment and observation to philosophical situations. What was the significance of the first two nightmares? Descartes believed the wind in the first nightmare represented an evil force that tried to take him to a place he didn't want to go, and the thunder in the second nightmare was the signal of the spirit of truth taking possession of his mind. Although the exact meaning of these nightmares cannot be known, they inspired Descartes to pursue an entirely new method of philosophical thought.

Throughout his life, the nightmares of author Robert Louis Stevenson (1850–1894) were an important inspiration for his writings. An only child who tended to be sickly, Stevenson remembers "the unnatural activity of my mind after I was in bed at night."

He recalls "waking from a dream of Hell, clinging to the horizontal bar of the bed with my knees and chin together, my soul shaken, my body convulsed with agony." Stevenson was afraid of the dark and anything associated with the night—loud and threatening winds, moonlight, even the stars in the sky.

In an essay entitled "A Chapter on Dreams," Stevenson described how he was often terrified at the thought of falling asleep and "struggled valiantly" to stay awake. "But his struggles were in vain; sooner or later the night-hag would have him by the throat, and pluck him, struggling and screaming, from his sleep."

As he grew older, Stevenson came to welcome his nightmares, since they often provided the plots and scenes for his stories. Late in 1885, Stevenson wanted to write about the good and evil sides of man but was unable to think of a story line. Then one night he had a particularly vivid nightmare in which he screamed so loudly and horribly that his wife, Fanny, woke him up.

In that graphic nightmare, Stevenson dreamed of a good doctor who transformed himself into an evil and violent man by taking a mysterious powder concoction. The details of the nightmare were so specific that Stevenson wrote the first draft of the story in only three days.

When his wife suggested the piece was more an allegory (a fictional story or poem that symbolizes something else) than entertainment, Stevenson burned the first draft and wrote a second improved draft in three additional days. The result was *The Strange Case of Dr. Jekyll and Mr. Hyde,* published

I heard a noise downstairs, so I went down and saw a masked man looking straight at me. The man started walking toward me. I tried to run, but the man was too fast and caught up to me. He grabbed me and then BOOM! I was shot, but the second the bullet hit me, I woke up.

Joseph Baddour, 11 years old

in 1886, which dealt with the total transformation of a good man into his evil counterpart.

[Hyde] put the glass to his lips and drank at one gulp. A cry followed . . . his face became suddenly black and the features seemed to melt and alter . . . "O God!" I screamed, and "O God!" again and again; for there before my eyes—pale and shaken, and half fainting, and groping before him with his hands, like a man restored from death—there stood Henry Jekyll!

Although additional nightmares influenced and inspired Stevenson's other writings, *The Strange Case of Dr. Jekyll and Mr. Hyde* is considered by many to be his finest work.

The 18th century composer and violinist Giuseppe Tartini (1692–1770) wrote his most famous compositon after experiencing a nightmare about the devil. One night, Tartini had a terrible dream in which he had sold his soul to Satan himself, who had emerged from a bottle. When the devil criticized his violin playing, Tartini gave him the instrument and was amazed to hear Lucifer play a beautiful sonata.

The composer woke abruptly from his nightmare and immediately reached for his violin in an attempt to reproduce the devilish music he had heard. Although Tartini could not recall the melody, he did remember the sounds of a strange double-quaver and repeated trills, and he used these as the basis for his composition. The result was the "Devil's Trill Sonata" which some critics have called "one of the most imaginative and innovative [violin] pieces" of the century.

The well-known English poet Samuel Taylor Coleridge (1772–1834) often had nightmares of every variety. He once wrote to a friend, "The Night is my Hell, Sleep my tormenting Angel . . . my frequent Night-Screams have almost made me a nuisance in my own House."

One night in 1798, Coleridge had a vivid nightmare in which he composed hundreds of lines of poetry while simultaneously visualizing the poem's unusual fantasy images. When he awoke, Coleridge attempted to write down the poetry but could only remember 54 lines. What emerged was the poem *Kubla Khan,* one of his most famous works.

In each of these cases, nightmares proved to be more helpful than harmful to the dreamer. Learning to use nightmares creatively can be useful and exciting, and makes them seem less frightening. Read on to discover how to control or even eliminate your scary dreams!

Taking Control of Your Nightmares

Nightmares, like all dreams, tell you things about yourself. They are unique stories created by your subconscious that deal with your own particular thoughts, feelings, fears, and relationships. They are windows into your mind.

If you want to take control of these disturbing dreams, you must look through these windows, not try to ignore them. You must face up to the things that scare you and then learn more about them. You are less likely to be afraid of something you know about!

Dream researchers and psychologists have figured out a number of ways for people to deal with their nightmares. The following techniques have helped many succeed in controlling, preventing, and even eliminating a recurrence of disturbing nightmares. Some techniques may work better for you than others.

Drawing

Author Anne Sayre Wiseman believes that nightmares are messages about fear, and that "fear lets us know we need to protect or strengthen ourself." In her book *Nightmare Help,* Wiseman has devised a self-help system especially for young people who are reluctant to talk or write about their fears.

First, step back from the nightmare and draw it on paper, as if you were an observer.

Next, change the picture to make it safe. For example, if there's a monster or a scary animal chasing you, draw a cage or a wall around it. Maybe a superhero will fly to your rescue, or a police officer or a parent will rush in to help you.

Draw whatever will make you feel safe and comfortable. If your nightmare is about a fire, draw firefighters with water gushing out of their fire hoses. If bugs are the problem, draw bug spray. Drowning? Why not try an inner tube or a life jacket.

Now that the nightmare is safe, try to talk about it. Talk to the monster who's chasing you. Afraid to talk directly? Draw a telephone in the picture. What do you think it would say? Why do you think you're afraid of fires, or bugs, or swimming? Think back into the experiences of your life to get clues.

Nightmares can teach you about yourself. Try to listen to what the picture tells you. What is the message of the nightmare? How can you be in control and feel more powerful? What can you learn from your nightmare?

Writing

Dreaming is easy, but for many people it's the remembering that's difficult. Many sleep experts recommend keeping a journal or a notebook by the side of the bed along with a pen or a pencil to write down nightmares as they occur. You can even use the *Nightmare Journal* at the end of this chapter.

Upon awakening, don't get up, but focus immediately on any nightmares you have had. If you don't remember one right away, relax. Let your mind wander and you might recall something. If you do, reach for your journal and, while still in bed, write it down.

Record every detail—images, words, actions, and characters. Don't get out of bed until you've written as much as you can remember. Even a simple thing like walking to the bathroom can cause you to forget important details of the nightmare.

Throughout the day, something may remind you of your nightmare. Add more facts and images to your journal as you remember them.

Go back over the written account of your nightmare. Try to determine what all things mean. Are they symbols for something else? Why would they appear in your nightmare? Could they be related to people or things in your everyday life? Are they connected to past experiences?

If certain people are in your nightmare, share it with them. By talking with others, you may gain valuable insight and understanding into the meaning of your nightmare.

Imagery Rehearsal

This technique, described by doctors Barry Krakow and Joseph Neidhardt in their book *Conquering Bad Dreams and Nightmares,* has been successful in decreasing and even eliminating nightmares. It basically involves changing the nightmare into a more pleasant experience and then focusing on imaging (or imagining) the new dream in your mind. It is simple and has worked successfully for many nightmare sufferers.

For example, you wake up suddenly after a horrible nightmare. A scary-looking man carrying a knife ran angrily after you down the street. The man was about to stab you when you woke up terrified.

Lying in bed, you are so disturbed by the experience that you can't get back to sleep and are afraid you'll have the same nightmare again if you do.

You try imagery rehearsal by changing the nightmare in your mind into a happier experience. You begin to concentrate and focus on the pleasant images of the new, changed dream. In the new dream (which you can change in any way you like), you find yourself with several good friends, walking at night in your neighborhood. Your golden retriever is tagging along, and every so often you throw the ball for the dog to fetch. You laugh and joke with your friends and have a great time. At one point a strange-looking man passes by, but he says hello and you realize it's your neighbor from up the block.

By concentrating on the image of the changed dream, you will soon find yourself feeling more relaxed and getting sleepy. The next day, focus on the changed dream in your mind three more times, spending at least five minutes in total concentration each time.

Krakow and Neidhardt advise imaging a changed dream for at least three straight days after a nightmare, three times each day. If you have a new nightmare, repeat the process. Change the nightmare to be more pleasant, then image the changed version several times a day.

According to Krakow and Neidhardt, some people can cure their nightmares after only one or two days of imagery rehearsal. Others may need weeks or even months. The important thing is to teach yourself to imagine and concentrate on a happy, enjoyable image, which in itself can be a stress-reducing and relaxing activity.

You may decide to use one, two, or even all three of the techniques described in this chapter to understand, eliminate, and prevent your disturbing nightmares. Good luck and pleasant dreams!

Keep this *Nightmare Journal* within easy reach at your bedside, along with a pencil or a pen. Use it to record details of any nightmare you remember in the morning.

Don't forget to stay in bed until you've written as much as you can recall. Sharing your scary dream with someone may help to jar your memory. You can add to your *Journal* throughout the day as you remember additional facts. Have fun!

Nightmare Journal

Glossary

ANXIETY—distress, uneasiness, apprehension

AUTHENTICATED—determined as genuine

AVERTED—prevented, turned aside

CHANDELIER—a multibranched light fixture that hangs from the ceiling

CONCOCTION—a mixture of different ingredients

CREDIBILITY—the quality of being believable

DEBRIS—remains, ruins, rubbish

DIFFUSED—spread out, distributed

DISTRESS—pain, anxiety, sorrow, trouble

DORMANT—inactive, as if asleep

EQUATORIAL—pertaining to the regions near the earth's equator (midpoint)

EVACUATE—to leave, vacate, empty

EXALTED—elevated, glorified, of high station, noble

EXTRASENSORY PERCEPTION (ESP)—special abilities and knowledge that extend beyond the five senses

FACET—aspect, feature, view

GENUINE—real, honest, sincere

INEVITABLE—unavoidable, inescapable

INFINITE—unlimited, endless

NREM SLEEP—non-rapid-eye-movement sleep when dreams do not occur

PHILOSOPHY—the study of the principles or truths of a particular branch of knowledge

PRECOGNITIVE—knowing about events before they actually happen; *see premonition*

PREMONITION—an advance warning of an event; *see precognitive*

PRIMITIVE—old-fashioned, earliest of its kind

PROXIMITY—nearness in place, time, or relation

PSYCHIC—a person sensitive to certain things that are caused by something other than the known forces of nature (the supernatural)

PSYCHOLOGY—the science of the mind and human behavior

RECURRENCE—the act of occurring again, repeating

RELUCTANT—unwilling, disinclined

REM SLEEP—rapid-eye-movement or dream sleep

SUBCONSCIOUS—beneath consciousness, the mental processes of which the individual is unaware

SUBSEQUENT—following after something, in order

SUFFRAGE—the right of voting

SYMBOLISM—representing things by symbols, standing for or meaning something else

VAIN—useless, worthless, futile

Bibliography

Balfour, Graham. *The Life of Robert Louis Stevenson.* New York: Charles Scribner's Sons, 1901.

Berry, Joy. *Every Kid's Guide to Understanding Nightmares.* Sebastopol, CA: Living Skills Press, 1987.

Brook, Stephen. *The Oxford Book of Dreams.* Oxford, England and New York: Oxford University Press, 1983.

Coxhead, David and Susan Hiller. *Dreams—Visions of the Night.* New York: Thames and Hudson, Inc., 1976.

Editors of Time-Life Books. *Dreams and Dreaming.* Alexandria, VA: Time-Life Books, 1990.

Editors of Time-Life Books. *Realm of the Iroquois.* Alexandria, VA: Time-Life Books, 1993.

Farga, Franz. *Violins & Violinists.* New York: Frederick A. Praeger, 1950, 1969.

Gibson, Walter B. *Dreams.* New York: Constellation International, 1969.

Green, Carl R. and William R. Sanford. *The Mystery of Dreams.* Hillside, NJ: Enslow Publishers, 1993.

Guiley, Rosemary Ellen. *The Encyclopedia of Dreams.* New York: Crossword, 1993.

Hartmann, Ernest. *The Nightmare: The Psychology and Biology of Terrifying Dreams.* New York: Basic Books, Inc., Publishers, 1984.

Hennessy, James Pope. *Robert Louis Stevenson.* New York: Simon and Schuster, 1974.

Hirsch, S. Carl. *Theater of the Night—What We Do and Do Not Know About Dreams.* Chicago, IL: Rand McNally & Company, 1976.

Holzer, Hans. *The Psychic Side of Dreams.* St. Paul, MN: Llewellyn Publications, 1992.

Kellerman, Henry, Editor. *The Nightmare—Psychological and Biological Foundations.* New York: Columbia University Press, 1987.

Kincher, Jonni. *Dreams Can Help—A Journal Guide to Understanding Your Dreams and Making Them Work for You.* Minneapolis, MN: Free Spirit Publishing, 1988.

Kirsch, James. *The Reluctant Prophet.* Los Angeles, CA: Sherbourne Press, Inc., 1973.

Krakow, Barry, M.D. and Joseph Neidhardt, M.D. *Conquering Bad Dreams and Nightmares.* New York: Berkley Books, 1992.

Kutz, Dr. Ilan. *The Dreamland Companion.* New York: Hyperion, 1993.

Miller, Gustavus Hindman. *10,000 Dreams Interpreted.* New York: Rand McNally & Company, 1995 (24th printing).

Parker, Julia, and Derek Parker. *Parker's Complete Book of Dreams.* London: Dorling Kindersley, 1995.

Quinn, Adrienne. *Dreams of History That Came True.* Tacoma, WA: Dream Research, 1987.

Roseman, Marina. *Healing Sounds from the Malaysian Rainforest.* Berkeley, CA: University of California Press, 1991.

Schwarz, Boris. *Great Masters of the Violin.* New York: Simon and Schuster, 1983.

Shulman, Sandra. *Nightmare.* New York: Macmillan Publishing Co., Inc., 1979.

Smith, Norman Kemp. *New Studies in the Philosophy of Descartes.* New York: Russell & Russell Inc., 1963.

Stevenson, Robert Louis. *The Strange Case of Dr. Jekyll and Mr. Hyde and Other Famous Tales.* New York: Dodd, Mead & Company, 1961, 1979.

Stewart, Kilton. "Dream Theory in Malaya," from Tart, Charles T. *Altered States of Consciousness.* New York: John Wiley & Sons, Inc., 1969.

Ward, James. *Dreams and Omens.* London: Foulsham and Co. Ltd., 1991.

Wiseman, Anne Sayre. *Nightmare Help.* Cambridge, MA: AnSayre Press, 1986.

Index

A

B

C

D

E

F

H

R

S

T

W